SHARKS

Special thanks to Louis Garibaldi, Director of the New York Aquarium,
for his help as text consultant.

Revised Edition

Copyright © 1989, 1979 by Burton Albert, Jr., and Platt & Munk, Publishers, a division of
Grosset & Dunlap, Inc., a member of The Putnam Publishing Group, New York. All rights
reserved. Published simultaneously in Canada. Printed in Singapore. Library of Congress
Catalog Card Number: 88-81711 ISBN 0-448-09077-5   A B C D E F G H I J

CHARLES

and WHALES

By Burton Albert

Illustrated by Pamela Johnson

Grosset & Dunlap • New York

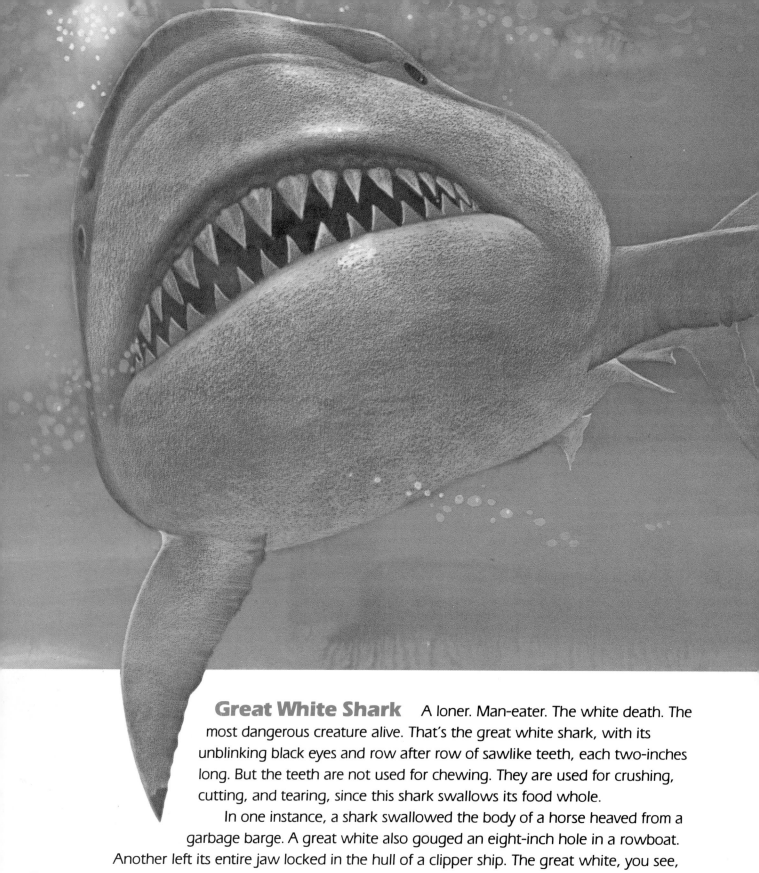

Great White Shark   A loner. Man-eater. The white death. The most dangerous creature alive. That's the great white shark, with its unblinking black eyes and row after row of sawlike teeth, each two-inches long. But the teeth are not used for chewing. They are used for crushing, cutting, and tearing, since this shark swallows its food whole.

In one instance, a shark swallowed the body of a horse heaved from a garbage barge. A great white also gouged an eight-inch hole in a rowboat. Another left its entire jaw locked in the hull of a clipper ship. The great white, you see, stops at nothing!

Angel Shark   As sharks evolved over millions of years, they divided into two groups. The larger group became the cigar-shaped sharks. The other turned into flat-bodied skates, or rays. With winglike fins, they ''fly'' through the water.

Today's rare angel shark looks like a ray. It grows to four or five feet—about as long as your outstretched arms. When seen, it is often close to shore, partly buried in the sand.

Port Jackson Shark   Unlike most sharks, the Port Jackson has two kinds of teeth. With pointed teeth near the front of its mouth, it picks up shellfish to eat. Then it crushes the shells with its flat rear teeth.

The Port Jackson looks most like the first kind of shark that ever lived.

Nurse Shark   With long whiskers drooping from its nostrils, the nurse doesn't look like a shark. And unlike most sharks that need to keep moving in order to breathe, a resting nurse can pump water through its gill slits while lying still. During the day, it sleeps under a shallow, sea-bottom ledge. The nurse shark, which preys on spiny lobsters at night, is itself a tempting target for skindivers. They mistake it as harmless and grab hold of its tail for a free ride. Surprise—they get a bite from a grumpy "nurse"!

Blue Shark   More "great blues" roam the ocean than any other large sharks. Slimly built, a blue can sprint up to 45 miles per hour and cruise for many miles at half that speed. But it rarely nears the shallows. Instead, it travels offshore in packs of hundreds and even thousands. It feeds on herring, mackerel, and other fish as well as birds and dead whales. Many people believe that blue sharks have also devoured victims of downed planes and disabled ships.

Basking Shark

"Helm alee! A monster...a sea serpent!" sailors once shouted. And that's exactly what five or six basking sharks look like when they swim nose to tail. This habit has also won them the name elephant shark, a name that fits their size as well. They love to cruise near the sunny surface of the water. There, they sift tons of tiny sea life, called krill, through the gill rakers that stretch across their throats.

Lemon Shark   This dangerous, sharp-eyed shark prefers saltwater creeks and bays. There, it probably feeds on skates, rays, and small fish. From time to time it may even attack swimmers.

When any shark breaks a tooth, a replacement grows right in. But a young lemon shark loses so many teeth, it replaces whole sets of teeth every eight or ten days!

Dusky Shark   What a bite this shark has! When one of these eight-footers sinks its teeth into a dolphin, the strength of its press is enormous. Every square inch of the surface where the teeth strike gets as much pressure as if three or four elephants were standing on it!

Thresher Shark   Because it has a small mouth and small teeth, the thresher doesn't depend on its bite to catch food. It uses its long, sickle-shaped tail to thrash the water and round up schools of herring and other small fish. By rushing through the school of fish, the shark stuns them, then devours the dazed fish that cannot swim away fast enough. At times, the thresher can toss a fish into its mouth with the simple flick of the tail that gives the thresher its nickname—sea fox.

Large and Small Black-Tipped Sharks

These sharks are acrobats. When hooked on a fish line, they leap and spin in mid-air—a breath-taking sight.

The small black-tipped shark has bigger eyes than its larger cousin, but both can see and smell the shrimp boats they trail. Schools of these sharks pierce the nets or feed on the trash-fish shoveled overboard.

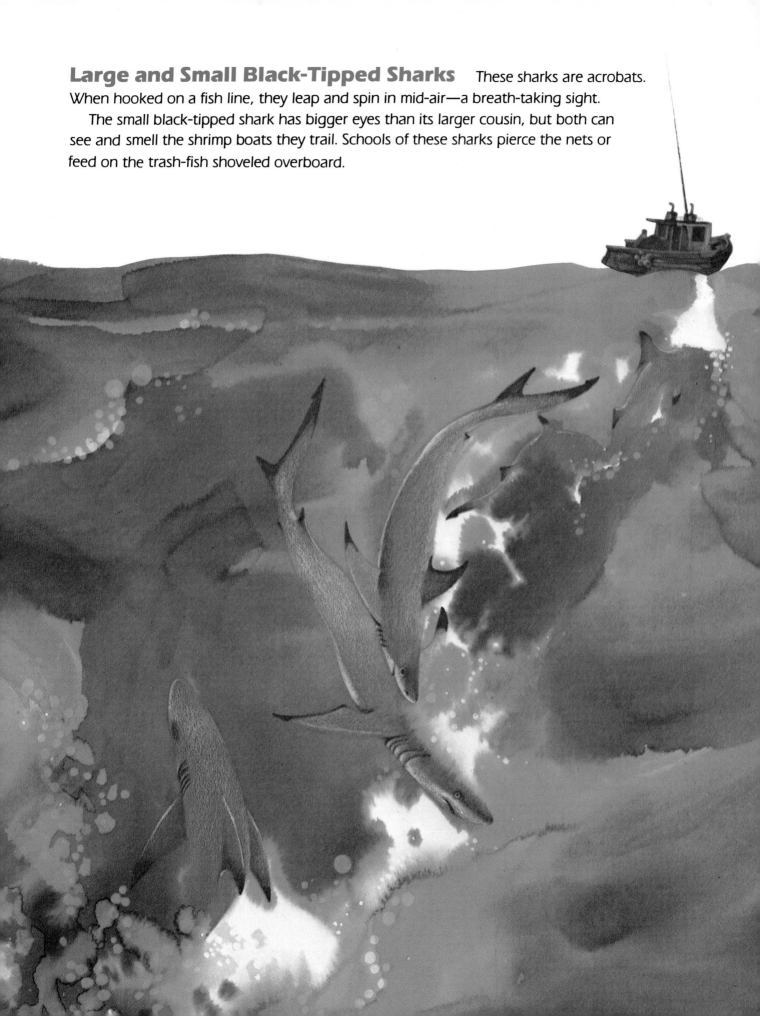

Bull Shark   This slow-moving shark feeds close to shore. It also travels up river from the ocean into a large freshwater lake in Central America. Pilot fish glide along its side.

Bull sharks are known to swim 3,000 miles up the Amazon River. However, they must return to the ocean to breed and have their young. Some experts say bull sharks kill more people than do any other kinds of sea creatures.

Great Hammerhead

Just look at that face and head! It's five times wider than the rest of the shark's body. Even the eyes are set three feet apart. So, too, are the nostrils. Yet this distance seems perfect for protecting the shark from the dangerous and painful tail whip of a stingray, the hammerhead's favorite meal.

Greenland Shark   Among sharks, the Greenland rules the Arctic waters. It spends all of its life there and feeds on squid, salmon, and seals. It is sometimes called a "sleeper" because it moseys about to save energy in the freezing cold.

Unless they have to, Eskimos will not eat a Greenland. They must prepare it very carefully. Its flesh is slightly poisonous and can make a person feel drunk and sick.

Sleeping Shark   These sharks were found in Mexican caves. There, where the water is less salty, they lie motionless as if asleep.

A woman who studied this kind of shark believes that the brackish water may loosen the barnacles and other tiny animals that grow on the shark's body. The remora, a fish that rides the shark, gives its host a "cleaning" by eating the loosened animals.

Dogfish   "What pests!" a fisherman will tell you. These small sharks not only eat crabs, but they feast on boating equipment, too. There are 30 different kinds of dogfish. Few grow beyond three feet—a yardstick long. Seldom does one weigh more than 10 pounds.

   The female spiny dogfish carries her babies for two years before they are born. That's one of the longest periods for any animal with a spinal column. Another kind of dogfish gives off its own light. Scientists understand how it is done, but why is another mystery of the sea.

Mitsukurina   When Japanese fishermen caught this extremely rare fish off the coast of Yokahama, they called it "goblin shark." And a stranger, more prehistoric-looking creature never swam the seas. Mitsukurina has a long, dagger-shaped horn growing out of its forehead.

Wobbegong Shark Look closely and find the animal with the tassel-trimmed mouth. It is hard to see the wobbegong or carpet shark. Its marblelike markings match the floor of the sea, where it spends its day. Because a swimmer cannot see the shark either, it is easy to step on.

A wobbegong's favorite food is crayfish. It will even invade a crayfish post, or trap, to reach this ocean-bottom treat.

Swell Shark   The swell shark grows only as long as a yardstick. It likes to lurk in beds of seaweed. But if something disturbs this shark, it wedges its body into a crevice and inflates with water so it cannot be pulled out.

Sand Tiger Shark   Sand tigers travel in schools, linger near beaches, and swallow food whole—such as eels or crabs. They can suck air into their stomachs, which enables them to swim slowly without sinking.

   Sand tigers are the only known creatures to have babies that kill each other before they are born. The first one hatched from thousands of eggs eats the other babies inside the mother's body.

Mako Shark From cobalt blue above to snow-white below, the mako is a beautiful shark. It is also one of the fastest in the world. Just think of how it must race to catch its natural enemy, the broadbill swordfish. This fish pierces the water at speeds of up to 60 miles an hour with the mako in close pursuit. That's faster than most cars zoom by on an expressway.

Usually, though, the mako feeds on schools of squid, herring, and bottom fish. When caught on hook and line, it whirls and spins and leaps as high as a cabin cruiser.

Porbeagle   In ancient Greece, children teased other children by saying a monster will eat them. They gave their make-believe creature the name porbeagle, which meant "man-eating monster."

The porbeagle shark is very swift and acts much like the mako but prefers colder waters. It follows and feeds on schools of mackerel.

Tiger Shark   This night prowler loses its tigerish brown stripes as it ages. It often trails fishing boats, tears into nets, and feasts upon the catch. During an attack, schools of tigers seem to go crazy. They may even bite the rudder and anchor of a boat.

A tiger shark will gobble anything—from a whole sea turtle to a 30-foot roll of roofing paper. In fact, one shark downed some canned goods, a leather wallet, a coil of wire, a sack of coal, a driver's license, and an 18-pound tom-tom. This creature is among the most feared of the man-eating sharks.

Whaler Shark   More than 100 years ago, sailors on whaling ships in Australia named this shark. It would trail the wash of waves and rip away parts of the harpooned whales that the men were towing ashore. Today, in that part of the world, this 700-pounder rivals the tiger shark as the deadliest fish. Its victims often include humans.

Whale Shark   This shark, sometimes called a checkerboard shark, is the giant of the fish world. It is as long as a trailer truck and weighs as much as ten large horses. Its jaws can open wide enough to swallow humans. But, strange as it may seem, the whale shark feeds only on the smallest of sea life—shrimp, plankton, and baby fish, which it filters out from the water as it swims along.

Sometimes the whale shark "stands" straight up and puts its mouth just above the sea. Then it pumps up and down to rinse out its mouth. As the water swirls and swishes, little fish dart in and out of the whale's mouth to feed on the discarded food particles.

Sperm Whale

"Thar she blows!" bellowed sailors of old. They could tell by the forward-slanting spout that a great sperm whale was swimming up ahead. A huge mammal, it was hunted mainly for heating and lighting oil.

A sperm's head measures about one-third the size of its body and contains a brain that is the largest of any animal on earth. The sperm whale can grow as long as 60 feet. It can also stay underwater for 90 minutes and dive deeper than any other whale. The sperm whale has 50 to 60 teeth, all in its lower jaw. The teeth fit into openings in the upper jaw and are used for attacking sharks, fish, octopus, and giant squid.

Greenland Right Whale

Some whales, like the sperm, have teeth. Others have baleen, which is also called whalebone and is made of the same material as your fingernails.

As a baleen whale skims the surface of the sea, it gulps a huge amount of water that swells its throat. Then the whale closes its mouth and squirts the water out through its baleen. The baleen traps tiny sea animals that the whale eats.

The Greenland has 700 of these baleen plates hanging from its upper jaw. Each plate has feathery edges.

Long ago, whalers named these sharks which lived only in the Arctic. They were slow-moving, and so easy to catch and kill, that today hardly any of these great baleens are left.

Great Right Whale   This big-headed hulk wears a bumpy bonnet. It is made of horny, rough skin and has creases filled with whale lice. The cavelike mouth is filled with over 500 or more baleen plates.

Great rights usually travel in twos. They prefer cool waters close to island clusters. Because of the large number that have been slaughtered, the great right may be the rarest of all the great whales.

Pilot Whale   The pilot whale plays follow-the-leader. Wherever the biggest, oldest pilot male goes, so go thousands of others. They'll follow him blindly, even getting stranded ashore, where they whimper like babies and die.

One of the very few all-black whales, the pilot weighs three tons. It has small, pointed teeth and feeds mainly at night on squid, octopus, and similar sea animals. When it spouts, it also barks—a sound that people enjoy at water shows where pilot whales sometime perform.

California Gray Whale   These hairy, cigar-shaped creatures put on a show at sea. People watch while schools of hundreds sail along the west coast to spend winter in the lagoons of Baja, California. To get there, the whales travel 13,000 miles from the Arctic. Some scientists think the whales do not rest or eat during the three-month journey.

Sometimes, if a whale comes too close to the shore, it gets stuck in the shallow water. It doesn't panic but simply waits for the tide to rise and rides out to sea with it.

Humpback   What an athlete! Despite its size and weight—45 feet and 50 tons—the humpback rolls, leaps, swims on its back, and even turns complete somersaults in the water.

What a singer, too! It produces long, slow, complicated songs that last from six minutes to half an hour. To some listeners, the songs sound like the squeaks of a rusty hinge. To others, it's the pleasant sound of bagpipes and oboes. Yet the "beautiful music" may end if the killing of the humpback continues.

Killer Whale   Twelve, two-inch teeth in each jaw of the killer whale are set like this 🦷. When this eight-ton creature attacks, its teeth interlock for gripping and tearing.

If the killer circles and closes in on a great whale, its teeth go first for the victim's tongue. Then the killer lets the victim bleed to death before chomping on the carcass. Killers also feast on porpoises, seals, and other fish, and even dead whales being towed by factory ships. In an aquarium, however, the killer is gentle, probably because its handlers feed it well.

Common Dolphin   This member of the whale family usually performs in the waves of ships. There it leaps and frolics in schools of up to 200 dolphins.

    The dolphin feeds on sardines, herring, squid, and crabs. And at times it taunts a sea turtle or a fish the way a cat plays with a mouse.

    Dolphins show great concern for each other. If one is sick or wounded, others will hold it above water with their heads—for several days if necessary—so the sick dolphin can breathe as it gets well. Likewise, a mother dolphin becomes very concerned about her newborn. She will not let it wander more than ten feet away. At birth she may choose another female to become the baby's "aunt."

Bottlenosed Dolphin   Bottlenosed dolphins are excellent performers in water shows and movies. They are longer and fatter than common dolphins. But like all dolphins, the bottlenosed makes use of *echolocation*. That is, the dolphin gives off a number of different sounds—from those humans cannot hear to those that sound like clicks. Vibrations from the sounds bounce back through the water and tell the dolphin the size and shape of any object in its path.

Risso's Dolphin   This friendly creature has a bulging forehead that makes it look like a pilot whale. It is also larger than most dolphins. Sometimes it grows to 13 feet.

   The Risso has been known to make regular trips with boats. The most famous Risso was Pelorus Jack. He guided the ferry from Wellington to Nelson, New Zealand through a body of water called Pelorus Sound. He did this each day for 30 years!

Susu   In the muddy Ganges River of India, where this small five-foot dolphin lives, hardly anything can be seen. So the susu is nearly blind. It depends on its pointed snout to dig up dinner. A susu is named for the noise it makes as it breathes.

Amazon River Dolphin   With very tiny eyes, very big cheeks, and a very long snout, this South American whale cannot see downward. But it can see upward. So this animal, which is not much larger than a susu, swims upside-down at the bottom of the river to get its food. The Amazon River dolphin is also called the pink porpoise because of the color of its belly.

Yangtze River Dolphin
Some people think this creature may be blind. It lives only in the Yangtze River in China. With nearly 140 teeth, it feeds on fish, shrimp, crabs, and the like. Its dorsal, or rear, fin gives this strange whale its more common name—white flag dolphin.

Atlantic Humpback Dolphin
This small whale is the only species in West Africa that enters into rivers in order to feed on mud-living fish.

Common Porpoise

To tell a dolphin from a porpoise, look at its teeth. The dolphin has cone-shaped teeth. A porpoise has spade-like teeth.

One of the smallest of all whales, the porpoise grows about as long and as heavy as a Great Dane or an Irish wolfhound. Although it acts like a dolphin, the porpoise likes to travel in small groups. It also prefers to linger near a coast.

Sounds from porpoises are many and varied. One sound is given off by the strongest porpoise in the group. The signal seems to mean, "Stay away from that fish. It's mine!"

Finback Whale

Longer than most houses and heavier than a dozen elephants, the finback is the second largest whale. Its two blowholes produce a spout as high as a giraffe. Sometimes this graceful mammoth leaps straight out of the water and splashes on its side in a thundering roar.

The finback, an endangered whale, is the only whale with such odd coloring. Its lower left jaw is black. The lower right is white. Its 250 to 450 pairs of baleen plates are blue-gray on the left and pale yellow on the right. Each day the baleen plates sift enough krill to equal 36,000 hamburgers!

Minke Whale

In the cold waters where it likes to spend its summers, the minke whale might be seen resting its head on an ice float. In fact, this whale goes closer to the South Pole than any other whale. It can grow as long as two vans and weigh as much as five middle-sized cars.

Alone or in small schools, it often follows ships and dives under them. This habit, however, is increasing the number of minke deaths. Some of the ships are on the prowl, ready to torpedo harpoons into the sides of these playful creatures.

Narwhal   The male narwhal has a tusk that looks like that of the unicorn, the mythical horse with a horn. But the tusk is really the upper left tooth grown out eight or nine feet. Some experts think the tusk is used for fighting or chipping air holes in the icy waters where the narwhal lives. Others think the twisted tooth may be used to dig food from the sea bottom, to spear fish, or to attract females. Its pale gray coloring gives this 12- to 20-foot creature its name. Narwhal means "corpse whale."

Northern Bottlenosed Whale   This 10-ton creature can deep-dive for up to a half hour. It spends summers in the Arctic and winters in warmer waters. The bottlenosed has only one pair of teeth. They are in the lower jaw. Its mouth has a lining, however, that looks like pink terry cloth. This nubby texture helps the bottlenosed whale hold on to its favorite meal—the thrashing, slippery squid.

Beluga Whale The only completely white whale is the beluga. It is most often found in shallow coastal waters in the Arctic Ocean. It can swim under the ice and use breathing holes made by seals. With 36 to 40 teeth, it feeds on fish, squid, cuttlefish, and crabs. Although it may travel in groups of 12, at times it may roam with larger herds numbering 800 to 1,000. The beluga is preyed upon by the killer whale and is a hearty dinner for the polar bear, too.

Sei Whale   Each year in Norway the sei appears at the same time as the seje, the pollack that gives the whale its name. Although it can grow as long as three station wagons and weigh as much as six of them, the sei is a swift swimmer. It can sprint at speeds of up to 35 miles an hour. And after a 10-minute dive, it can spout water as high as a one-story house.

The sei feeds on krill, sardines, and other fish. Its baleen has fringe as fine as silk. Unfortunately, because so many blue and finback whales have been killed, whalers in some countries are turning to the sei. Now its life is endangered.

Bryde's Whale   The Bryde's whale looks like the sei's twin. A close examination shows, however, that it is more streamlined than the sei and has three ridges on top of its head, rather than one.

On each side of the Bryde's jaw are 250 to 290 baleen plates. They are short, wide, and thick. They sift sardines, mackerel, and shoalfish from the warm ocean waters where the Bryde likes to roam. Schools of 100 or more are an amazing sight!

Blue Whale   This is the largest animal ever. It grows as long as a railroad car and as wide as a two-story house. It weighs as much as 20 or 30 elephants. No wonder it uses more than 700 baleen plates to sift four tons of krill a day!

The whale's heart weighs as much as 20 six-year-old children. Blood vessels leading from the heart are tunnels as big around as fire hydrants.

A baby blue is hefty. Each day it drinks half a ton of milk from its mother and gains 220 pounds!

Until now, a blue whale has usually lived for 100 years. But if the killing of the blue continues there may be none left to live that long again.